AI

MW00941344

for Us

care for busy couples

101 free ways for couples
to enjoy more love,
attention, and
togetherness
in 30 seconds.

Alice Langholt, MJS

Edited by Rayna Langholt

ISBN: 1507683634
ISBN-13: 978-1507683637

DEDICATION

I dedicate this book to the person who introduced me to
real love, and who helps me learn more about it every day
of my life – my husband, Evan. Thank you for loving me,
and for being my partner on this incredible journey.

HOW TO USE THIS BOOK

You will need 30 seconds. That's all.

Start at the beginning, or turn to a random page. Each page has a title, a benefit, and simple directions. Read and complete the task on the page.

Or, if you know that you are in the mood for a communication-enhancing, self-reflective, or time-together-oriented task, use the Index at the back of the book to choose one that fits your interest.

Doing the tasks in this book will give you and your partner a chance to learn about each other, grow closer, express appreciation, have better communication, and value each other in new and meaningful ways.

People are busy. Working on the relationship can take a back seat to a full schedule. This book will help you strengthen your bond in just 30 seconds a day, whenever you want. And, it works.

These 30 second tasks will bring about benefits which last far longer. *A Moment for Us* will help if you use it alone to improve your part in the relationship, or if you and your partner each try the different tasks inside.

Feel good about this 30 second time. Just trying the tasks in this book means that you want to have a stronger relationship, even if your time is severely limited. That intention is all you need to get started.

Take a 30 second Moment for Us. Let these moments help you and your partner nurture a strong, loving relationship.

Just for Today

Make sure to say, "I love you" to your partner today.

Love Goals

Couples can become closer when they have goals for the relationship.

Separately, write 3 things you would like to improve in your relationship.

Then, share and discuss steps to meet these goals.

Doing this will help you understand your partner's needs, and allow you to share yours too.

Make an effort to work towards them now that you know what they are.

Ask Yourself

Sit quietly, breathe for 10 seconds, and ask yourself:

What can I do to make today special for my partner?

When the idea comes to you, do it!

Conversation Starters

Sharing something new together increases bonding. Do this task together with your partner.

For the next 30 seconds, take turns answering this question:

What helps me relax the most?

Wisdom Break

Access and express some of your accumulated wisdom. Surprise! You're wise!

In a notebook, write your answers to:

3 things I've learned about how I like to receive love.

Share your answers with your partner, or just reflect on them.

Whisper, "I love you."

There's something sensual about whispering in your partner's ear.

Kiss your partner's ear and whisper, "I love you."

Say, "Thank You."

Feeling appreciated goes a long way in keeping people together.

Think of something about your partner for which you feel sincerely grateful.

Tell him or her what it is.

Open to More Love

Love begins within and affects all who you encounter.

Try this for the next 30 seconds:

1. Put both hands on the center of your chest.
2. Close your eyes.
3. Breathe slowly, feeling your heart energy warm your whole being and radiate outward.
4. Envision a big light shining from your heart, filling your body and extending outward to the world.

Notice how your interactions feel today.

Send a Loving Text

Reestablish a loving bond when you are
away from each other.

Send a text message to your partner at a
random time during the day today.

Say, "You're awesome!" or, "I'm thinking
of you," or, "I love you." (Or choose a
different endearment.)

Doing this will brighten the day for
both of you.

Make Eye Contact

Often, we get caught up in our day-to-day "stuff", and forget to really give attention to each other.

Acknowledge each other now by looking into each other's eyes for a full 30 seconds.

Don't try to send any messages or do anything more than that. If you want to laugh, laugh. If you want to smile, smile. Enjoy giving and receiving attention.

The eyes are the windows to the soul.

Write 3 Love Notes

Brighten your partner's day by taking three sticky notes and writing the following on each: "I love your _____." Fill in the blank spaces with three things that you love about your partner.

Then, stick each note in a different place where your partner will find it and feel loved.

Just for Today

Surprise your partner with a gift.

Big or small, it doesn't matter. It's the thoughtfulness that will matter most.

Ask Yourself

Sit quietly, breathe for 10 seconds, and list:

3 things I want more of in my relationship with my partner.

Reflect on how you can best communicate your desires, and work toward them together.

Conversation Starters

Sharing something new together increases bonding. Do this task together with your partner.

For the next 30 seconds, take turns answering this question:

Who do you admire most and why?

Say Affirmations

To realign yourself with positive energy, attract more goodness into your life, and increase optimism, say each of these aloud and with feeling:

I am a loving, compassionate partner.

I express kindness in my words and actions.

I am grateful for my relationships.

Take an Us-Selfie

We can get so busy with daily life that we only take pictures of the two of us together on formal occasions.

Take your cell phone or camera, get together, and take some quick shots of both of you now.

Set the picture as your phone, Facebook, or computer desktop picture today.

Make Time for Each Other

Time alone together doing something you both enjoy increases bonding and creates memories.

In the next 30 seconds, plan and schedule a date and get it on your calendar.

Prioritizing your relationship is an important validation of its importance. The anticipation of the event will give you something to look forward to.

It doesn't have to be fancy; it just has to be focused on time you spend being together.

Appreciate Differences

You and your partner are individuals in your own right. You have your own interests, and that makes you interesting and well-rounded. Appreciating that each partner has interests and making it a point to learn something about them can help strengthen your relationship.

Can you name 3 facts about your partner's hobby or special interest?

If not, make it a point to learn from your partner what he or she finds most fascinating about the subject.

Cuddle

There are few things that bring people together like cuddling.

For 30 seconds or more, wrap your arms around each other and focus on sharing the loving feeling between you.

Do a Chore Together

Sharing the chores can become a bonding experience, and more fun, as you accomplish something for the good of the household together.

Choose a chore and do it together.

Enjoy the time and attention that your relationships gets by accomplishing this task.

Doing, Being, and Bringing

Write a note to your partner that begins, "Thank you so much for _____" and **list three things** you want to express your appreciation to your partner for, **according to the following:**

- Something your partner **does**,
- **A quality that you love** in your partner
- Something your partner **brings to your life.**

Just for Today

Make it a point to smile at your partner.

Sincerely think of what makes you feel good about being together. Reflect that feeling as you look at your partner and genuinely smile because your partner is in your life.

Enjoy your partner's response.

Ask Yourself

Sit quietly, breathe for 10 seconds, and list:

3 things I want less of in my relationship with my partner.

Reflect on how you can best communicate your desires, and work toward them together.

Conversation Starters

Sharing something new together increases bonding. For the next 30 seconds, take turns answering this question:

How do I define love?

Just for Today

Use good manners all day.

Good manners means, of course, making a point to say, "please" and "thank you." It also means offering kind gestures, being helpful, and it could also mean doing your best to be pleasant to be around.

It is common for couples to get "extra comfortable" with each other, and stop using manners.

Notice how your day changes when you make the effort to look nice, smell nice, speak in full sentences, and keep body noises private.

Wisdom Break

Access and express some of your accumulated wisdom. Surprise! You're wise!

In a notebook, write your answers to:

3 things I've learned about how I express love.

Sneak a Kiss

Spontaneity and shows of affection are wonderful at bringing couples closer.

Sometime today, surprise your partner with a kiss at an unexpected moment.

Affectionate Gestures

Affectionate gestures bring couples closer. There are many ways to express love and affection.

Here are some ideas, but add your own ideas to the list, too:
- playing "footsie,"
- caressing your partner's hair,
- winking, raising your eyebrows up and down with a smile,
- a quick kiss on the back of the neck or forehead,
- holding hands, or mouthing "I love you."

Choose one or more to do today!

Ask Yourself

Being a couple means you can watch each other grow and be a support for each other's growth.

Think about three ways in which your partner has grown since you met him or her. Write them down.

Share your list with your partner.

Your partner may be surprised to find out what you see and appreciate in him or her.

Energetically Connect

Doing these actions with intention can deepen your bond:

For 7-10 seconds each:
- Place a hand gently on each other's foreheads and intend to be more intuitive to each other's needs.

- Look into each other's eyes.

- Place a hand on each other's heart center (center of the chest) and intend to flow more compassion to each other.

- Hold both of each other's hands, palms together, and intend to be more supportive to each other.

End with a loving hug.

Untie Yourself

Stress from the day can keep a hold on you, even when you are home with your partner.

Take 30 seconds and **make a conscious choice to release the stress before you come into the house, allowing yourself to fully enjoy the experience of being together.**

Suggestion: imagine the stressors of your day as ropes around you. Untie yourself and drop them around your feet. Step out of the ropes and in the door.

Just for Today

Choose to focus on patience in all of your interactions.

Take a breath before reacting, and let your partner finish speaking, as you listen intently, before you answer.

Ask Yourself

Sit quietly, breathe for 10 seconds, and write your answer to:

What are the qualities of an ideal love relationship?

Afterward, consider this question:

How you can bring more of what you want into your life now, and increase those qualities you already have?

Conversation Starters

Sharing something new together increases bonding. For the next 30 seconds, take turns answering this question:

If you could return to one moment in your life, which would it be?

Dance Together

Moving together to music is a wonderful and expressive bonding experience.

Put on a song that fits your mood and dance together for 30 seconds (or longer!)

Exchange Compliments

Giving and receiving compliments goes a long way in bringing couples closer.

Tell your partner something you sincerely appreciate about him or her, and then receive a compliment from your partner.

You may be surprised at what you are told.

Be sure to say, "Thank you!"

Forgive Something

In every relationship, there are disappointments, resentments, and disagreements. Forgiving and releasing are key to keeping the relationship healthy.

Think of something, big or small, which your partner did or said, that you feel ready to forgive and release.

Imagine that event floating out of the place inside you where it was held. Send it up into the atmosphere like a helium balloon, until it can no longer be seen.

Replace the place it used to occupy with love and compassion.

Now do the same exercise to forgive yourself for something you regret doing or saying to your partner.

Gentle Touch

Loving touch is an essential part of intimacy in a relationship.

Today, make it a point to caress your partner's hair, face, shoulder, hand, or back. First, think of the love you have for your partner. Then, infuse your touch with that emotion.

It will translate as you offer the touch.

Give a Toast

A toast is a wonderful, impromptu way to express gratitude and appreciation.

At your next meal or snack together, hold up your drink, and toast something nice.

Even simply saying, "To our love!" and clinking glasses together will be met with surprise and delight and give you a fun way to express gratitude for the love you share.

Have an Electronics-Free Evening

Real connection happens when both people are fully engaged in the moment. This includes conversation.

Plan an evening that involves only the two of you, undistracted by phones, computers, and TV.

Light a candle. Talk. Connect.

Afterward, reflect on how this experience affected your evening.

Use a Sweet Nickname

Do you have an endearing nickname for your partner? Something that reminds you of a special moment you shared, or maybe just "sweetheart"?

Today, use a sweet nickname that will make your partner feel special and close to you.

Just for Today

Do something considerate and
caring for your partner
as a gesture of love.

Ask Yourself

Sit quietly, breathe for ten seconds, and list:

3 things I would like my partner to do more often.

Then, ask for them.

Communication is the key to getting your needs met.

Conversation Starters

Sharing something new together increases bonding. For the next 30 seconds, take turns answering this question:

What would you like to know about me that you don't already know?

Wisdom Break

Access and express some of your accumulated wisdom. Surprise! You're wise!

In a notebook, write your answers to:

3 things I've learned about communication.

Share a Love Poem

Poetry uplifts the soul by reminding us of the beauty of language.

Choose a love poem and read it to your partner.

If you don't have a book, go online to http://www.poemhunter.com/poems/love and choose what speaks to your heart!

Just for Today

No criticism. If you feel like saying something critical, find something positive to say instead.

Notice the way choosing your words carefully gives you time to decide what's really important.

(Bonus: Try this task on the same day as your partner.)

Say Affirmations

To realign yourself with positive energy, attract more goodness into your life, and increase optimism, say each of these aloud and with feeling:

I see the best in my partner.

I am honest with myself and my partner.

My relationships enhance my life.

Plan Together

For the next 30 seconds, brainstorm together activities, trips, or adventures you want to take with your partner in the future.

Making the list together is the first step toward making them happen.

Then, put a star next to those you can do within the next year and a half.

Send Love and Light

The relationship between you and your partner is an energetic one.

Energy flows back and forth between you like a cord of light.

For these 30 seconds, imagine that cord, and flow a big stream of love from your heart to your partner's, as the cord between you glows brighter.

Notice how this exercise makes you feel.

Do this exercise together or separately.

Save for Something Special

Together, choose a special vacation, outing, or item that you want to save for.

Then, make a plan to put a certain amount aside each week towards that goal. Commit to the plan and keep it.

You will both enjoy the anticipation of bringing your goal into reality, and then enjoying it together.

By doing this, you're investing in your relationship, and prioritizing it.

Just for Today

Let your partner talk without interrupting, and listen without trying to think of what to say next until your partner is finished.

Give your partner your full attention and see what a difference it makes in your communication.

Ask Yourself

Sit quietly, breathe for ten seconds, and list:

3 things I would like my partner to do less often.

Then, gently and sensitively share this list with your partner.

Communication is the key to getting your needs met.

Conversation Starters

Sharing something new together increases bonding. For the next 30 seconds, take turns answering this question:

If all jobs paid the same amount of money, what would you choose to do?

Warts and All

Love means being accepted even with your flaws.

Think of your flaws. We all have them. Think of your partner's.

Take this 30 seconds to realize that **when you love each other with your flaws, you love the true person, not the illusion of an unflawed version of the person.**

Deeper connection comes from the trust of allowing yourself to be known and loved, warts and all.

Write an Acrostic Poem

Write your partner's name vertically.

Then, across each letter, write a phrase or adjective describing your partner's best qualities, a fun memory, or something you love about your partner.

Give it to your partner afterward.

What a thoughtful gift!

Share Something New

There are an unlimited number of things to learn about the other person in your relationship, no matter how long you've known each other.

Think of something that you can share about your life that you haven't yet, and tell your partner about it.

It could be an event from your childhood, a favorite poem or book, or what your younger self wanted to be when you grew up.

Pick something to share, and share it. The openness will bring you closer.

Water Your Garden

Some people spend too much time comparing their lives to those of others.

There's a saying that the grass is greener where you water it.

If you place your focus on nurturing and being grateful for the relationship that's yours, the need to compare will be replaced by the joy of loving what you have.

Give Each Other a Foot Rub

A foot rub helps you feel good, refreshes tired muscles, and activates a flow of energy to your whole body and mind.

The nerves and energy points in the foot connect to all major organs and areas of the body, as well as emotional energy centers. Giving each foot a quick massage can revitalize your partner's energy flow in a short amount of time, and is a beautiful way to nurture each other.

- Sit facing each other, holding your partner's foot.

- Massage each other's feet firmly for 30 seconds. (Longer if you want!)

Ask an Open-Ended Question

Feeling listened to and heard goes a long way in bringing people together.

Instead of asking, "How was your day?" try, "What was the best part of your day?" Or, choose another open-ended question and **really listen** to your partner's answer.

Sing to Your Partner

There's a special sort of vulnerability that comes from singing to another person.

A measure of trust goes along with the act of singing a love song to your partner, and is a gift in itself along with the song.

It doesn't matter how good a singer you think you are, take a little loving risk and sing 30 seconds of a love song just for your partner.

Do this one on one, in person, or as a surprise voice mail. It will express love, trust, and make your partner feel special.

Just for Today

Tune in to non-verbal signals in communication, such as body language, hand gestures, and facial expressions. And, become aware of your own as well.

Pay special attention to the way people around you use non-verbal communication, and what they are saying.

What messages are you getting, and what messages are you sending through your non-verbal signals?

How does adapting this kind of focus change the way you communicate?

Ask Yourself

Write 5 qualities that you consider to be ideal in a partner.

Then, ask yourself which of these qualities you bring to the relationship.

Consider: what can you do to strengthen each quality in yourself?

Conversation Starters

Sharing something new together increases bonding. For the next 30 seconds, take turns answering this question:

What books have influenced your life?

Wisdom Break

Access and express some of your
accumulated wisdom.
Surprise! You're wise!

In a notebook, write your answers to:

3 things I've learned
about my partner.

Hold Hands

The act of holding hands is a loving gesture that brings people together.

For 30 seconds, hold hands and really focus on feeling the touch of your partner:
- the sensations,
- pressure,
- and closeness involved in this connection.

Just for Today

Respect means treating someone like he or she is important.

In a relationship, respect needs to go both ways.

Today, choose to treat your partner with respect. Let that choice be reflected in your words and actions.

Notice how making this choice affects your communication.

Kiss Good Morning, Goodbye, and Good Night

Make it a habit to kiss each other at least these three times per day.

Each time, kiss as if it's the first time - with the intention for a gentle expression of love and attraction.

Spice it Up

Breaking from routine adds interest and fun.

Today, choose to either:
- wear something special,
- make a new recipe,
- try a new food,
- music,
- or activity.

Show your partner what you've tried, so you can share the experience.

Reminisce

You got together because there was an attraction. The qualities of the other person triggered something in you which led to love.

Use these 30 seconds to remember together the moments that were the spark of your relationship, and revisit them together.

Watch the Sunset Together

Taking time to appreciate nature together is romantic!

When it's dusk, step outside together and watch the colors in the sky change. Hold hands or put your arms around each other.

Alternately, watch the sunrise or gaze at the moon and stars.

Just for Today

Whatever we place our attention on grows stronger.

For today, with that in mind, give the most attention to positive thoughts, positive feelings, and gratitude.

Notice how that changes your day and communication. Allow this positive attitude to affect your interactions with your partner.

Ask Yourself

Sit quietly, breathe for 10 seconds, and write your answer to:

What parts of myself do I hide from my partner, and why?

Vulnerability and trust make a relationship stronger. Allowing yourself to be vulnerable and trusting that your partner will accept you despite your flaws and mistakes is challenging, but can strengthen the bonds of your partnership.

What can you share with your partner that will help your partner know the real you? Write whatever comes to mind, and save it for your reflection.

Conversation Starters

Sharing something new together increases bonding. For the next 30 seconds, take turns answering this question:

What are you most proud of?

Say Affirmations

To realign yourself with positive energy, attract more goodness into your life, and increase optimism, say each of these aloud and with feeling:

I have the power to create the life that I want.

I am sensitive to my partner's needs.

I prioritize my relationships and they help fulfill me.

Cook Something Together

Cooking together can make a meal you share become even more special.

In this 30 seconds, choose a recipe that you'd like to make together. Plan when you'll make it, and follow through.

Enjoy the process of the quality time the activity offers, and the rewards of sharing the meal itself.

Golden Love

The "Golden Rule" for love is: **treat your partner as your partner wants to be treated.**

Do you know how your partner prefers to receive attention? Is it through touch, words of affirmation, helpful gestures, time together, or thoughtful gifts?

Imagine yourself in your partner's shoes, choose one of the previous categories, and then today, be sure to offer attention in that particular way today.

Support Each Other's Alone Time

We all need time for ourselves now and then to stay balanced. Gift each other an hour or two alone to use as you wish.

Support your partner's alone time by guarding it as if it was your own. Don't call or text your partner. Answer the phone, and do whatever you can to give your partner this uninterrupted time.

Your partner will do the same for you when it's your turn. **In this 30 seconds, coordinate your calendars and schedule your and your partner's alone time.**

Hug Each Other

Hugging has been shown to have healing effects, because it releases endorphins in the brain which are responsible for happiness, love, and healing.

20 seconds is the minimum needed for this effect, hug each other and hold that hug for 30 seconds, for that extra 10 seconds of benefit.

Let yourself be immersed in that loving space and soak it in.

Then, smile at your partner and say, "Thank you!"

If You Could

Engage your imagination in adding more to your life.

Imagine you could telepathically share your feelings and thoughts with your partner.

For these 30 seconds, imagine yourself showing him or her all that you want to share.

Afterward consider: What did you share, and how can you communicate the same message through your words and actions?

Know Your Triggers

We all have things that "push our buttons," making us feel immediately irritated or angry.

In these 30 seconds, write down 3 of yours.

Then consider how you could avoid the tendency toward immediate reaction the next time they get pushed. Write your ideas next to each trigger on your list.

Just for Today

Often, we can be distracted by our own concerns, and miss subtle gestures of love that are offered to us.

Today, **watch for signs of love that are offered to you.** Whenever your partner says or does anything that's a loving gesture, for example, a loving look, a light touch, or a smile, recognize and accept it with gratitude.

Flirt with Each Other

Partners want to feel attractive to each other, especially in long-term relationships. One of the best ways to express that you're still attracted to your partner is to flirt.

Today, put your attention on wooing your partner. Do those flirty things that you did when you were trying to attract and impress him or her.

Have fun with it!

Conversation Starters

Sharing something new together increases bonding. For the next 30 seconds, take turns answering this question:

Where is the most beautiful place you've ever been?

Wisdom Break

Access and express some of your
accumulated wisdom.
Surprise! You're wise!

In a notebook, write your answers
to:

3 things I've learned from past relationships.

Choose Compassion

All reactions come from fear or love. When negative-sounding words are said to you, **try to discern the need behind the words,** and respond with compassion in trying to meet the need.

For example, is your partner feeling insecure or unappreciated? If you can respond with what your partner needs (compassion and reassurance), the situation will be diffused and resolved in a loving space.

Think about the last time this happened. Then ask yourself, "How could I respond to this from a place of love?" Imagine this situation as it could have been instead. As you go about your day, try to **consciously choose love.**

Laugh Together

Laughing is a light way to remember how much fun it is to be together.

For the next 30 seconds, think of an experience you shared that was funny, and talk about it. Enjoy revisiting that moment and laughing.

Notice the way enjoying the experience of laughing together brings you closer.

Light a Candle

Anywhere can become a romantic setting with the right touches.

Light a candle and eat together by candlelight. Even a drink or dessert together can become a romantic moment.

Notice how your mood shifts with this change in lighting.

Love Yourself First

We can be better at expressing love to our partner when we feel worthy of love ourselves.

Today, talk to yourself only as you'd talk to the person you cherish most in the world.

Ponder this idea for a moment. How will this plan change your usual self-talk and the way you treat yourself? Try it.

After you have done this exercise today, reflect on how you feel with your partner. What's different?

Express Pride

It always feels good to hear that our partner is proud of us.

Think of a reason that you are proud of your partner - maybe it's an accomplishment, or the gentle way your partner treats children or pets, or how attentive your partner is to his or her parents.

Whatever it is, be sure to tell your partner today that he or she makes you proud, and why.

Embrace Impulsivity

Unpredictability is exciting.

Do something unusual to surprise and delight your partner.

Ideas: leave a love note in the pocket of your partner's jacket, go to a new restaurant for dessert, see a play without knowing in advance what it will be about.

In these 30 seconds, choose one idea and go for it!

Just for today

No complaining.

If you feel like complaining, substitute the phrase, "At least it's not .... (something worse)" and let it go.

Notice the way your day changes when you lighten up.

(Bonus: Try this task on the same day as your partner does.)

Encourage Each Other

Do you know what your partner's dreams, goals, or aspirations are?

If not, ask.

If so, give your partner some sincere encouragement that will help him or her know you are supportive and believe that he or she can accomplish them.

Conversation Starters

Sharing something new together increases bonding. For the next 30 seconds, take turns answering this question:

What do you want to be remembered for?

Learn Together

Learning together gives you new things to talk about and enjoy as a couple.

Go online together and find a class in something that interests both of you. Sign up and take it!

Alternately, choose a book that you'll both read and discuss together.

Focus on Solutions

It can be tempting to agonize or assign blame when something goes wrong. But the fastest way to solve a problem is to focus on solving it.

Together with your partner, think of any problem or issue you are facing right now, and brainstorm possible steps to a solution.

This process will bring you together as a team and infuse appreciation for each other into the process.

Come back and review the plan you made whenever you need a reminder.

Have a Real Conversation

Asking an open-ended question invites a true conversation. The next step is to listen fully to the answer.

Instead of "How was your day?" ask, "What was the best part of your day?"

Try "What do you think about _____," or "How do you feel about _____" as conversation openers that can help you express that you care about your partner's thoughts, emotions and experiences by inviting your partner to share them.

Battle Together

Sometimes many things can feel irritating. It can be tempting to lash out and vent a list of complaints. However, it's seldom productive to do so.

Think of your list of irritations, and then choose only those which can really be changed for the better right now.

Then, take one that you selected, and enlist your partner's help in working on making it better - together.

Balance Each Other

This exercise is a good way to recognize the way your personalities support your relationship.

Often, a couple will have qualities that seem to be opposite in each partner, yet they balance the other.

For instance, if one partner is impulsive, the other is grounded. If one is extroverted, the other is introverted.

Think of your partner, and list 3 ways you balance each other. Write them down and share them with your partner.

Read and Share

When you learn something, and then share it with your partner, you have something new to discuss. Communication is freshened up by this activity.

Go online and search or surf until you find something you find interesting. Read it. Your partner should also do this activity.

Then, tonight, spend some time sharing what you found and learned.

If instead, you want to share what book you're reading, or something you heard on the radio today, feel free to substitute. **In this 30 second time, decide what you will share.**

Wisdom Break

Access and express some of your
accumulated wisdom.
Surprise! You're wise!

In a notebook, write your answers to:

3 things I've learned about love.

INDEX

ABOUT THE AUTHOR

Alice Langholt is a Reiki Master Teacher, the Executive Director of Reiki Awakening Academy School of Intuitive Development (ReikiAwakeningAcademy.com), and the founder of Practical Reiki, a strong, simple Reiki energy healing method.

Alice is the author of the award-winning book, *Practical Reiki for balance, well-being, and vibrant health, A guide to a strong, revolutionary energy healing method*, and *The Practical Reiki Companion* workbook, as well as a deck of cards, Energy Healing Cards, (also published as an app for Android and iOS devices). Alice also authored the *A Moment for Me 365 Day Self Care Calendar for Busy People*, and *A Moment for Mom* (AMoment4Me.com).

She's passionate about finding and teaching simple approaches to strengthening intuition and achieving holistic balance.

Alice lives with her husband and their four children in Gaithersburg, Maryland.

She teaches Practical Reiki and other holistic topics, and offers workshops on 30 second methods of self-care online and in the Washington, DC area.

Contact Alice by email at Alice@AMoment4Me.com.

CPSIA information can be obtained
at www.ICGtesting.com
Printed in the USA
LVOW12s0223290817
546778LV00001B/7/P